MW00563494

Silly Joke Books

SILLY JOKES
ABOUT
FOOD

by Michael Dahl

PEBBLE
a capstone imprint

Published by Pebble, an imprint of Capstone
1710 Roe Crest Drive, North Mankato, Minnesota 56003
capstonepub.com

Library of Congress Cataloging-in-Publication Data is available on the Library of Congress website.
ISBN: 9781977131607 (hardcover)
ISBN: 9781977154859 (ebook pdf)

Summary: A collection of food jokes for young readers.

Editorial Credits

Editor: Christianne Jones; Designer: Brann Garvey and Mighty Media; Media Researcher: Jo Miller; Production Specialist: Laura Manthe

Image Credits

Shutterstock: Abramova Elena, 10, milkshake, Alexiuz, 23, Ann Bulashenko, 3, 24, bergamont, Cover, banana, Bored Photography, 16, cupcake, Clara Bastian, 10, cow, Daniellart, 17, cake, Dirk Ercken, 20, frog, Elizabeth A.Cummings, 12, bubble gum, F. JIMENEZ MECA, 5, banana peel, FabrikaSimf, Cover, strawberry, Fortyforks, 9, peanut butter bread, Fotaro1965, 12, bubble, grey_and, 11, spoon, 18, fork, Gyorgy Barna, 18, cake, iamnong, Cover, broccoli, Ian Dyball, Cover, eyes, IndiTheater, 13, peanut, JeniFoto, 7, lemonaid, Jessica2, 4, sunblock, Jin young-in, 4, sunglasses, Kitch Bain, 11, cereal, Linda Parton, 7, thermometer, lunamarina, 9, jellyfish, M. Unal Ozmen, 20, fries, soda, Madlen, 13, nachos, Maks Narodenko, 7, lemon, MaraZe, 15, lettuce, MarcoFood, Cover, blueberry, Michael Vi, 14-15, track, Moises Fernandez Acosta, 6, bottle, MR.Silaphop Pongsai, 17, bear, New Africa, 5, slippers, RaksanstudioSStock, 6, tomato, Rich Carey, 9, jellyfish, S.Z, 12, train, SaGa Studio, 4, bananas, Smit, 11, snowman, souloff, design element, Stiva Urban, 19, StudioPhotoDFlorez, 14, vegetables, studiovin, 4, sunglasses, Svekrova Olga, 6, monkey, SweetLemons, 7, eyes, 14, eyes, 15, eyes, Thasneem, 21, blueberries, Timolina, 8, Twin Design, 16, teddy bears, VisionDive, 9, shark, Volosina, 6, tomato paste, Yeti studio, 15, chips, Zamurovic Brothers, 21, ghost

All internet sites appearing in back matter were available and accurate when this book was sent to press.

Printed and bound in China. PO4205

Table of Contents

HELLO!

FUNNY FRUIT

Why do bananas wear sunscreen?

They don't want to peel.

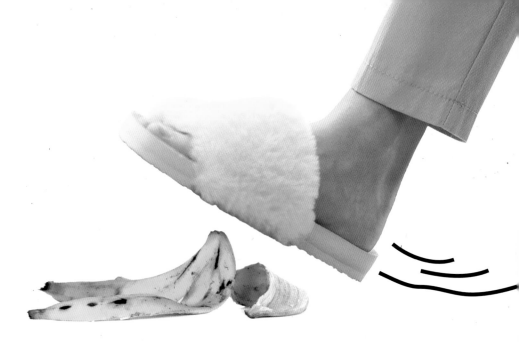

What do you call two bananas?

A pair of slippers.

Why did the apple go dancing with the prune?

Because it couldn't find a date.

Why was the strawberry late driving to work?

It got stuck in a jam.

Did you know you can use a key
to open a banana?

Yeah, a monkey.

How do you fix
a broken tomato?

Tomato paste.

SQUIRT

What do you give a sick lemon
to make it feel better?

Lemon-aid.

LOONY LUNCH

What did one plate say to the other?

Lunch is on me.

Why did the tortilla chip start dancing?

Because they put on the salsa.

What does a shark eat with peanut butter?

Jellyfish.

Why did the farmer make his cow jump up and down?

He wanted a milkshake.

"Waiter, will my pizza be long?"

"No, it will be round!"

Why can you never starve in the desert?

Because of all the sand which is there.

What do snowmen
eat for breakfast?

Frosted Flakes.

CHEWY CHUCKLES

How does bubble gum go on vacation?

It takes the chew-chew train!

CHEW CHEW

What did the shell
say to the peanut?

"I got you covered!"

MINE!

What do you call cheese
that doesn't belong to you?

Nacho cheese!

13

What did the little corn say
to the mama corn?

"Where's popcorn?"

Who won the vegetable race?

The lettuce. It's always a head!

What is fast, loud, and crunchy?

A rocket chip!

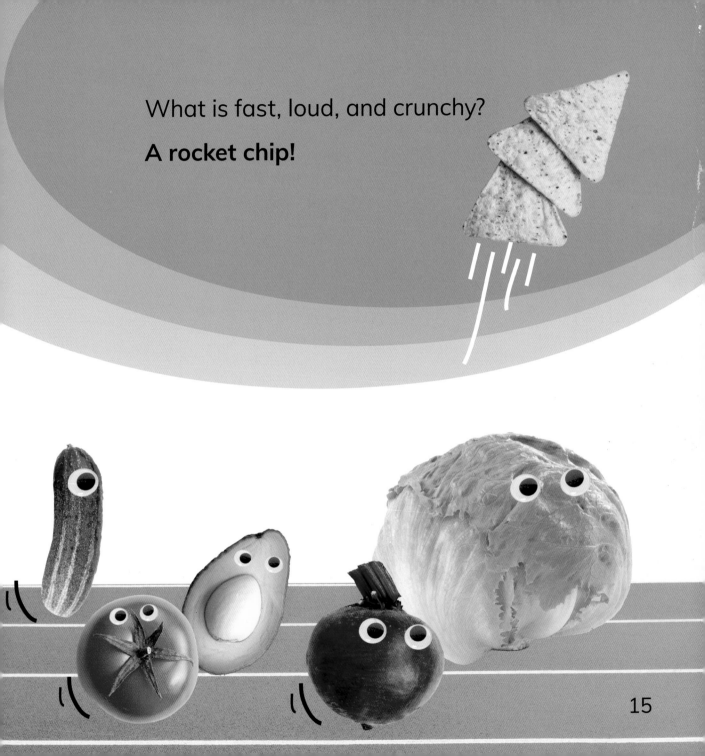

Why didn't the teddy bear eat dessert?

It was stuffed!

What fruit teases the others?

A ba-nana-nana-nana!

What kind of cake
do you get when
you eat too fast?

A stomach-cake.

What did the cake
say to the fork?

**You want a piece
of me?**

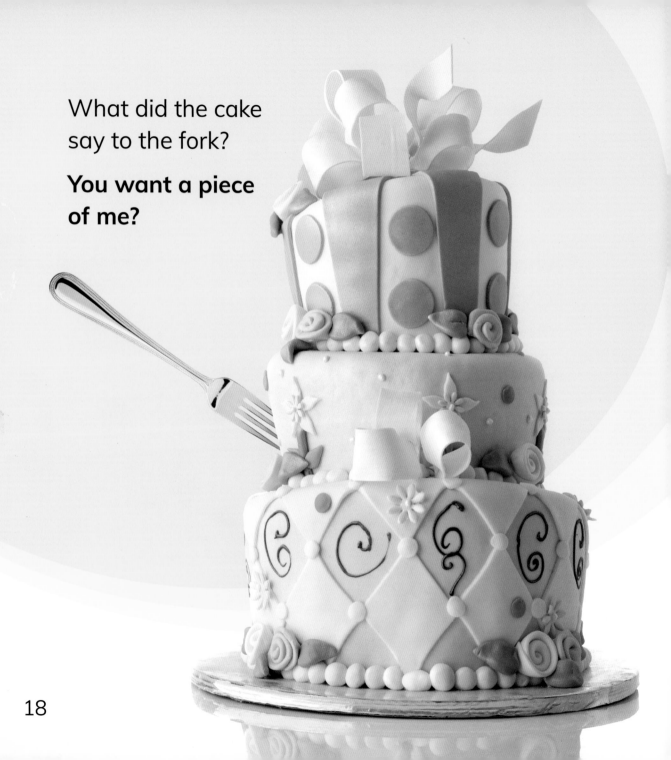

What happens when you tell an egg a joke?

It cracks up!

HA! HA! HE! HE!

Why did the cookie go to the doctor?

It was feeling crumby.

What is an astronaut's favorite food?

Launch meat.

What did the frog order for lunch?

French flies and a diet croak.

What is a cheerleader's favorite drink?

Root beer.

What is a ghost's favorite fruit?

Booberries.

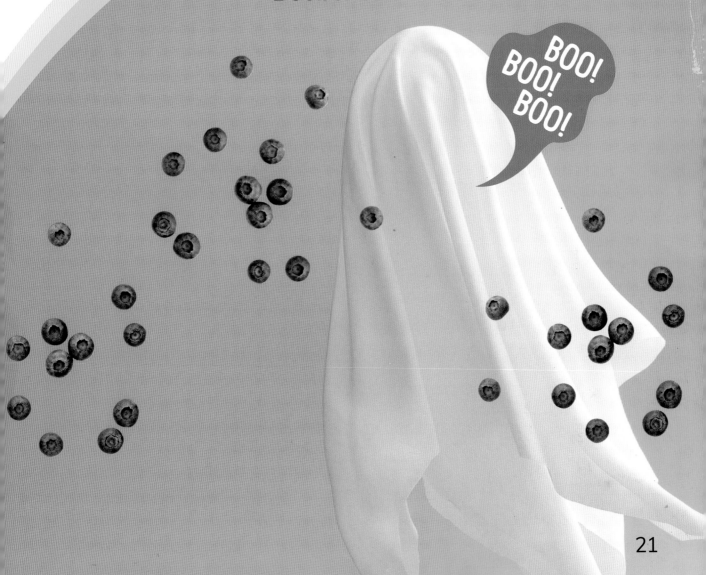

ACTIVITY: MENU MADNESS

What you need:

- paper
- markers
- crayons or colored pencils

What you do:

1. Make your own funny food menu. Fold the paper in half to make the menu.

2. Draw a picture of one funny food item on the front of the paper. Write the funny name of the item at the top.

3. On the inside, write down an appetizer, a main course, and a dessert.

4. Use funny words to name each food item. Include funny descriptions too.

5. Put the menu on the table and crack up your friends and family!

GLOSSARY

crumby (KRUM-ee)—not good

launch (LAWNCH)—when a rocket takes off into space

salsa (SAHL-suh)—a lively type of Latin American music

starve (STARV)—to run out of food and be very hungry

READ MORE

Dahl, Michael. *Scooby-Doo Food Jokes*. North Mankato, MN: Capstone, 2015.

Pellowski, Michael J. *Mega-funny Jokes & Riddles*. New York: Sterling, 2017.

Wing, Natasha. *Lettuce Laugh: 600 Corny Jokes About Food*. New York: Sterling, 2018.

INTERNET SITES

Enchanted Learning
www.enchantedlearning.com/
jokes/topics/food.shtml

Kidactivities
kidactivities.net/food-jokes-kids

THE END

INDEX